ALSO BY JOHN ASHBERY

POETRY
Turandot and Other Poems
Some Trees
The Tennis Court Oath
Rivers and Mountains
The Double Dream of Spring
Three Poems
The Vermont Notebook
Self-Portrait in a Convex Mirror
Houseboat Days
As We Know
Shadow Train
A Wave
Selected Poems
April Galleons
Flow Chart
Hotel Lautréamont
And the Stars Were Shining
Can You Hear, Bird
Wakefulness
The Mooring of Starting Out
Girls on the Run
Your Name Here
As Umbrellas Follow Rain

FICTION
A Nest of Ninnies (with James Schuyler)

PLAYS
Three Plays

CRITICISM AND ESSAYS
Reported Sightings: Art Chronicles 1957–1987
Other Traditions (Charles Eliot Norton Lectures)

CHINESE WHISPERS

CHINESE WHISPERS

POEMS BY

JOHN ASHBERY

FARRAR, STRAUS AND GIROUX • NEW YORK

Farrar, Straus and Giroux
19 Union Square West, New York 10003

Distributed in Canada by Douglas & McIntyre Ltd.
Printed in the United States of America
Published in 2002 by Farrar, Straus and Giroux
First paperback edition, 2003

The author gratefully acknowledges the following publications in which poems in *Chinese Whispers* first appeared, sometimes in slightly different form: *The American Poetry Review, Bard Papers, Conjunctions, The Germ, Green Mountains Review, The Harvard Advocate, Harvard Review, Hotel Amerika, jubilat, The London Review of Books, Nest, The New Yorker, The New York Review of Books, L'Oeil de Boeuf, The Paris Review, PN Review, Poetry, Poetry Review* (UK), *Raritan, Shiny,* and *The Times Literary Supplement*; also *Carcanet 2000: A Commonplace Book* and The Drawing Center's *Line Reading: An Anthology 2000–2001.*

"The American" was first published as a broadside by the Dia Center for the Arts on the occasion of John Ashbery and Robert Creeley's reading, 13 January 2001.

A number of these poems were included in the collection *As Umbrellas Follow Rain*, published in a limited edition by Qua Books, 2001.

The Library of Congress has cataloged the hardcover edition as follows:
Ashbery, John.
    Chinese whispers : poems / by John Ashbery.— 1st ed.
      p.   cm.
    ISBN 0-374-12257-1 (alk. paper)
    I. Title.

PS3501.S475 C48 2002
811'.54 — dc21

2002025016

Paperback ISBN 0-374-52880-2

Designed by Jonathan D. Lippincott

www.fsgbooks.com

10 9 8 7 6 5 4 3 2 1

This book is dedicated to
Ed Barrett, Olivier Brossard, Mark Ford,
Kenneth Koch, Ann Lauterbach, John Yau

and to my editor of thirty years, Elisabeth Sifton

CONTENTS

CHINESE WHISPERS

A NICE PRESENTATION

I have a friendly disposition but am forgetful, though I tend to forget only important things. Several mornings ago I was lying in my bed listening to a sound of leisurely hammering coming from a nearby building. For some reason it made me think of spring which it is. Listening I heard also a man and woman talking together. I couldn't hear very well but it seemed they were discussing the work that was being done. This made me smile, they sounded like good and dear people and I was slipping back into dreams when the phone rang. No one was there.

Some of these are perhaps people having to do with anything in the world. I wish to go away, on a dark night, to leave people and the rain behind but am too caught up in my own selfish thoughts and desires for this. For it to happen I would have to be asleep and already started on my voyage of self-discovery around the world. One is certain then to meet many people and to hear many strange things being said. I like this in a way but wish it would stop as the unexpectedness of it conflicts with my desire to revolve in a constant, deliberate motion. To drink tea from a samovar. To use chopsticks in the land of the Asiatics. To be stung by the sun's bees and have it not matter.

Most things don't matter but an old woman of my acquaintance is always predicting doom and gloom and her prophecies matter though they may never be fulfilled. That's one reason I don't worry too much but I like to tell her she is right but also wrong because what she says won't happen. Yet how can I or anyone know this? For the seasons do come round in leisurely fashion and one takes a pinch of something from each, according to one's desires and what it leaves behind. Not long ago I was in a quandary about this but now it's too late. The evening comes on and the aspens leaven its stars. It's all about this observatory a shout fills.

In collapsed mode the fish seem to ply downriver.
Evening settles in
with as many errors as usual. Too bad
they didn't ask my advice—I'd have told 'em
once more how the residuals taper off
into climate change.

Beer and pretzels is the one luxury here.
Tented figures walk the escarpment
behind which a luxury hotel is planned
for comic suicides in the next decade.

If all of us were one
again, how right life as usual would chime!
We can't keep combing out the old process
and have it rhyme,

neither can we rest at the table under the shade-
tree an anonymous donor provided.
We can only go on extracting fishhooks
from meanings that were intended to be casual.

Night settles briskly as with feather duster
and rag under arm, determined to be not too civilized.
It seems the sky left us
hanging, long ago, and now wants us undetermined,
untried sheep nosing out of mist.
Be thankful for all you haven't been, and could be
in a warier situation. For desk values. The shoehorn.

Our lives ebbing always toward the center,
the unframed portrait.

THE SLEEPING ANIMALS

I forget it. I've even
forgotten that I forgot
it. So go on with your
story, but make it
quick this time.

As if any admission were a cure . . .
You can thank me for that,
in fact you can thank me double for that.
We're both riding in the same direction,
and really, how much policing is necessary
to punish people after dark?

Night, the sleeping animals—
it all gets carted away,
sooner or later. The fife and drum
rebegin. It's here that narrative,
in our sense, implodes.
The shabby tale that was left
in the hangar starts to look better, gold
highlights in the corners of the eyes.

But for this to happen we have to trust
the narrator. We must stay vigilant.
The tale is multicolored, and jerks
back and forth like the tail of a kite.
If he was so smart, how come we're not dumber?
How come I can see into the epicenter,
brilliant little ball of cold? Still,
when it's over, it's, like, over.

The colonel returned to his senses.

DISCLAIMER

Quiet around here. The neighbors,
in wider arcs, getting to know each other.
The fresh falling away.
A sweetness wells out of the dark about now.
The explorer angles his telescope
at frigid violets on a settee.
A curate is near.

Frogs and envelopes join in the fun:
That was some joust! they say. Today we learned two things
too many: how to whimper, and the secret stasis of land.
Always, coming home
you pause before the little bridge, sigh, and turn ahead.
The real time of water gives you little wiggling room,
but it's all right, because it's all over.

Some dream accosted me on the turnpike. I felt straitlaced
for a moment, then remembered your threnody,
a cassation of bathtubs and violas d'amore.
It brought me to passion. I was able to turn back
with a clean slate, noting possible drifts
of meaning that disappeared as soon as
illuminated, then reemerged as from a fit of pique.

DISAGREEABLE GLIMPSES

After my fall from the sixteenth floor my bones were lovingly assembled.
They were transparent. I was carried into the gorgeous dollhouse and
placed on a fainting couch upholstered with brilliant poppies. My ship had
come in, so to speak.

There were others, lovers, sitting and speaking nearby. "Are you the
Countess of C?" I demanded. She smiled and returned her gaze to the
other. Someone brought in a tray of cakes which were distributed to the
guests according to a fixed plan. "Here, this one's for you. Take it." I
looked and saw only a small cat rolling in the snow of the darkened gutter.
"If this is mine, then I don't want it." Abruptly the chords of a string
quartet finished. I was on a shallow porch. The village movie palaces were
letting out. I thought I saw a cousin from years back. Before I could call
out she turned, sallow. I saw that this was not the person. Conversations
continued streaming in the erstwhile twilight, I betook myself to the
tollbooth. The pumpkin-yellow sun lit all this up, climbing slowly from
ankles to handlebar.

He had shaved his head some seven years ago. The lovers were bored then.
They no longer meandered by the brook's side, telling and retelling ancient
secrets, as though this time of life were an anomaly, a handicap that had
been foreseen. "In truth these labels don't go far. It was I who made a
career in singing, but it could just as well have been somewhere else."

Indeed? The dust was sweeping itself up, making sport of the broom. The
solar disk was clogged with the bristles of impending resolution. Which
direction did he say to take? I'm confused now, a little. It was my
understanding we would in joining hands be chastised, that the boss man
would be sympathetic, the sly apprentice unresonant as a squatter's tree
house. See though, it wasn't me that dictated . . .

that dictated the orbits of the plants, the viburnum at the door. And just as I
had called to you, the image decomposed. Restlessness of fish in a deodorant
ad. By golly, Uncle Ted will soon be here. Until it happens you can catch your

breath, looking about the walls of the familiar nest. But his flight was delayed for five hours. *Now* someone was interested. The travel mishaps of others are truly absorbing. He read from a large timetable and the helium balloon rose straight up out of the city, entered the region of others' indifference and their benighted cares. Can't that child be made to stop practicing?

In another life we were in a cottage made of thin boards, above a small lake. The embroidered hems of waves annoyed the shoreline. There were no boats, only trees and boathouses.

It's good to step off that steel carousel. The woods were made for musicianly echoes, though not all at once. Too many echoes are like no echo, or a single tall one. Please return dishes to main room after using. Try a little subtlety in self-defense; it'll help, you'll find out.

The boards of the cottage grew apart and we walked out into the sand under the sea. It was time for the sun to exhort the mute apathy of sitters, hangers-on. Ballast of the universal dredging operation. The device was called candy. We had seen it all before but would never let on, not until the postman came right up to the door, borne on the noble flood. Racked by jetsam, we cry out for flotsam, anything to stanch the hole in the big ad.

We all came to be here quite naturally. You see we are the lamplighters of our criminal past, trailing red across the sidewalks and divided highways. Yes, she said, you most certainly can come here now and be assured of staying, of starving, forever if we wish, though we shall not observe the dark's convolutions much longer (sob). Utterly you are the under one, we are all neighbors if you wish, but don't under any circumstances go crawling to the barrel organ for sympathy, you would only blow a fuse and where's the force in that? I know your seriousness is long gone, facing pink horizons in other hemispheres. We'd all blow up if it didn't. Meanwhile it's nice to have a chair. A chair is a good thing to be. We should all know that.

The last trail unspools beyond Ohio.

THEME PARK DAYS

Dickhead, they called him, for his name was Dong, Tram Van Dong. Carefully he slid open the small judas in his chest and withdrew a heart-shaped disk. It appeared to be cut from thicknesses of newspaper crudely stapled together. There was handwriting on one side, "spirit writing," he indicated with a motion of his head. Yet it all seemed for naught, ancient stock-market quotations or chalked messages on hoardings of the last century, with plus and minus signs featured prominently. *"O vos omnes,"* he breathed, "blown together like milkweed on the hither shore of this embattled plain, will your feet soon mean to you what once they did? I think not. Meanwhile the tempest brays, favor is curried, the taffetas of autumn slide toward us over the frosted parquet, and this loquat heart is yours for the dividing. Sailboat of the Luxembourg! Vibrations of crisp mornings ripple ever closer, the joiner joins, the ostler ostles, the seducer seduces, nor stirs far from his crimson hammock. Delphic squibs caparison the bleak afternoon and the critics love it, eat it up, can't get enough of it. 'More pap! More pap!' Have a care, though, lest what I tell you here trespass beyond the booth of our conniving. Yet it will spread, as surely as an epidemic becomes the element we have chosen to live in: our old infectious experiment."

IN WHATEVER MODE

"Tenderly," we thought. It estranged us a little.
A later kindness dissipates a sullen era's
awning. In the end we are all bores.
That's what it's for.

I plant my feet on the path
and look down a certain way. Surely, all this is coming
to an end, but, just as surely,
we know ourselves as affable.

A fine furor provoked it, storm swimming
in the weather vane. Two looked out.
"It's bait and switch time." Only if you mean it,
mean, that is, other stars.

The book hadn't been checked out all day.
"What are we to do for you . . ." A stranger,
ein Fremdes, shouted. The wide avenue of lamentation.

Others than you I've swatted
when it was impersonal. Now, it's you
I come back to. Out of love? The grown man whimpers.
Be careful with the vegetables, penises.

It was slowly she came down from the roof
to examine the withered nest in my hand, blunt thing.
I'd imagined you brutal, somewhat, under summer scarves.
Now the only way out is backward through the mess of cleaning.

Back to the back rows of the orchestra
where impatient silent citizens wait.
But it's not for us to let them go. Offer them a pear;
see how crystal the ditch is beside the main waterway.
Someone is coming to brunch.

And we can just leave it outdoors
all winter. That way, no one will mind.
It's the beauty of it, beauty of the fallen stone.

FROM THE DIARY OF A MOLE

Shoehorning in one's own tribute to crustiness is another life-form for him. Something then went out of us. In the pagan dawn three polar bears stand in the volumetric sky's grapeade revelation.

"Time to go to the thoughtful house."

They may not get you here, they may not get you there, they may not get you everywhere, but they will get you somewhere. Yet the proposition never came to a vote, was not voted on. You see the realism in it? No, of course you don't, for something else is still there, something to replace all of it in one block. Anent the spillway: His crimes are gorgeous but don't matter just now. Later

we will call him on them. When it subsides. That is, everything.

Just a teardrop of milk, thanks. Don't believe that rag. It inferred we were adolescents, once, that sex roared over us like a mudslide, leaving us. We were lost. So lost, in fact, that his mother didn't know me till I came out toward her, and she knew me and was not afraid, was glad in fact, for the rainbow late in the day in its foam of cloud, poised above the basin. Then I had a preshrunk sweater sent to him and asked if there was anything else. "Nothing, a fresh breeze." Still, leaves are asleep. The bears act as if no one's there. She curls up in the curlew's nest, weeping on its golden eggs. It took the savagery of centuries of animal conflict to bring us just short of this, and you, why have you done? Oh, I

don't much matter I guess. If that's all I'll be on my way. To the box in which savage handwriting is hidden, too dense for you to decipher, too lorn for a world to unravel just now, but like they say I'll be suing you. So really it's fine until Christmas I can stand it, a runt, I'll just go on blooming in my box, unaware of things sleeping pagans say about us, glad to crash, collapse the silk hat, garden's done and I'm all in and breathless for a breather. Come right in. What world is this.

TOO MUCH SLEEP IS BAD

I don't have a chronic cough.
Cats don't drool over me.
You can't listen to the change that's being monitored.
You can only participate in your life—

mutatis mutandis—

and they finally get it wrong.

THE BIG IDEA

Don't hit the bull's-eye.
The long winter festers,
day after unguarded day.
People are "shoveling out,"
night a monotony of stars and
other instances.

         The Big Idea
flourished for a while, then flagged
short of the summit.
The people's republics
went under like failing bakeries.
Always, in the shadows at the edge,
there was time to say this. And something.

Half past ten and the village
is out of order, shot through
with delirium tremens.
Tomorrow we shall arrive here
wondering what all the fuss was about.
Gawkers perpetuate the misquoted line.
One is all fingertips, one feels something
like at the border, a nowhere shine.

WHY NOT SNEEZE?

Oh dark days and punctual,
always backing into our alley,
feigning surprise for the umpteenth time:

Why don't you just go away?
Leave us to the land that binds
us and itself to present methods.
Leave the golf course simmering in light that has steeped
too long. It's the same with us, dull
on certain days.

Wake up, you're looking at this magazine.

A SWEET PLACE

How happy are the girls on the cocoa tin,
as though there could be nothing in the world but chocolate!
As though to confirm this, a wall stood nearby,
displaying gold medals from various expositions—
Groningen 1893, Anvers 1887—whose judges had had the good sense
to reward the noble chocolatiers. All love's bright-bad sweetness
gleams in those glorious pastilles.

But the empathy valve's

shut by someone—a fibrous mist
invades their stubborn cheeks and flaxen hair.
Time for the next audition.

Who to watch? What new celeb's dithering
is this, commemorated in blazing script?

The torches are extinguished in marl.
I will live in a house in the middle of the road,
it says here. No shit!
What did I do to deserve this? Who controls
this anger management seminar? They've had their way with me;
I am as I was before. Thank heaven! If I could but remember
how that was. *Always, it's nightfall
in a wood, some paths are descended,
and looking out over the ropy landscape, one sees
a necessity that was at the beginning.*
Further up there is fog. But it's nice being standing:
We should be home soon,
dearest, a dry hearth awaits us, and the indulgence of sleep.
What if I really was a drifter,
would you still like me? Would you vote
for me in the straw polls of November, wait for me
in the anteroom of December, embrace the turbulent, glittering skies
the New Year brings? Lie down with me once and for all?

The radio is silent, fretful; it bides its time
and the world forgets to consider. There is room to tabulate
the wonders of its sesquicentennials,
but the aftermath's unremarkable, picked
clean by a snarky wind.

Then I became as one who followed.

VIEW OF DELFT

The afternoon is slow, slower and slower
until a full stop is reached
long before anyone realized it.
Only the faintest nip in the air
causes these burghers to become aware
that their time is passing too, and then but fitfully.

Go stack those bricks over there.
See what the horse is doing.
Everything around you is waiting.
It is now apologized for.
The sky puts a finger to its lips.
The most optimistic projections confirm
the leakage theory. Another drop in temperature
is anticipated. It's all about standing still,
isn't it? That and remaining in touch with
a loose-fitting impression of oneself:
oneself at fifteen, out at night
or at a party in the daytime.
Oh sure, I knew it was me all along.

Then the sneezes got up to go.

POSTILION OF AUTUMN

A shower or two, and the old landscape
is good as new. A bit yellow in spots,
but that's what's called progress.
She hovers, lonesomely, like a zeppelin, over downcast
vales and trees, a free spirit, or something
like that.
          We'd reached the end of the grove,
it was time to turn back, to find what we'd left behind
waiting for us. And it was good to see the scraps
of pleasure assembling into a face. By and large conduits
of reduced gauge carry the fiber optics better,
the chatting, the suspense, lorries of debris
haunted by the sometime catchall of these cisterns. It was quite
cozy in the Midwest, he'd wanted to say, but never
understood how a question can just go out
like a pilot light, leaving the need rubbed and raw
in hankered-after faces.

THIS DEUCED CLEVERNESS

is what's the matter. Can't see without it.
Or was it, over the years of arrears,
swathed in a hoydenish privacy? No.
It's ours to deal.

The true crisis is only now coming to rest.
Birdie, on your tree,
I like you. Can't we be friends? Why is this awful
oxygen all that concerns us?
Seriously, I'd like you to come down.

On wings of windows, parties, songs,
comedy and mystery, the world drenches us.
It's the same world as before. Only time has exploded.
We mustn't draw many conclusions from that, only
keep our distance, as though the years mattered
to our education. We like us as we were before.
That's all right, no argument there,
no benediction either.

The month looks just as unsightly as before.
So who trained me to bring it inside,
pat it, make a fuss over it,
prepare its little dinner? It's not even ominous.
An ombudsman explained the nexus wasn't ours
to roost in, that we'd all be moving back in someday.

He laid it on the line and went home.
Said he needed a breather. The next day he was back
with a sheet of instructions. The neighbor dissented,
said it was all poppycock. There'd be no collective bargaining
without his input. As I'd noticed
on similar occasions, he left his cap in the hall.

Asked why he did so, the lout turned surly,
then stringently polite. It's your agreement,
he explained, you don't even have to sign it;
then took up the discussion at a farther juncture,
spoke in general terms
only vaguely related to the present situation.
Claimed it smacked of pettifoggery
and worse. But there would be peace along the way,
eventually—

If we shadows have offended
we'll replace the argument with the veil, again.
There can't be too many soft corners to lurch into.
The rooms have been spared the mindless tracking in
of guests. The carpets are fresh as moonlight,
I think, as in those ancient jalousie warehouses.

UNPOLISHED SEGMENT

Golden Fleece, where are you, Golden Fleece?
—Osip Mandelstam

The scribes are in agreement:
It would be a decade before the child is born
and two more before unhappiness
erects shyly into happiness
for a while till the suburban roadbed
is made over and grief laughs from oriels,
a billowing decline.

Roof down, it lay less urgent.
Panhandlers, virgins, tax collectors, the
self-medicating slime we were
overcame all that was
then. We said good night.

(Various pizzicati weighed in.)
I looked past the manger to the stuttering fields beyond:
Is it you who've come to take me to that place,
polish me,
in a world pressed into forgiving?

Then on four feet it turned,
as though having forgotten something,
came and presented it:

I said it was you all along.
I should have gotten up under the eaves, when thunders
yawned in the new day.
Perhaps I was too old, or not yet
old enough to undertake a new stage
of "life's journey," another episode.

But the sea gave repose.
He turned his face full to the leaves;
autumn caught him in the mouth,
slapped some worried sense into all of us.

The beginning of the middle is like that.
Looking back it was all valleys, shrines floating on the powdered hill,

ambivalence that came in a flood sometimes,
though warm, always, for the next tenant
to abide there.

MORDRED

Now I have neither back nor front.
I am the way certain persons are
who never tell you how they are
yet you know they are like you and they are.

I was preternaturally wise
but it was spring, there was no one to care or do.
It was spring and the sprinklers were on.

Bay, indentation, viscous rocks
that are somebody's pleasure. Pleasures that don't go away
but don't exactly stay,
stay the way they were meant to be.
I caught a winged one,
looked it firmly in the eyes:
What is your surmise? Oh, I only like living on,
the rest isn't so important to me,
not at all, if you wish.
But I do, I said. Then, well, it's like a clearing
in the darkness that you can't see. Darkness is meant for all of us.
We grow used to it. Then daylight comes again.
That's what I mean when I say about living
it could be going on, going somewhere else,
but it's not, it's here, more or less.
You have to champion it, then it fights for you,
but that isn't necessary. It will go on living anyway.
I say do you mind I'm getting tired.

But there is one last thing I must know about you.
Do you remember a midnight forge
around which crept the ghosts of lepers, who were blacksmiths
in a time persistently unidentifiable, and then you went like this?
You remember how the hammer fell slowly
taking all that song with you.

You remember the music of the draft horses
they could only make against a wall.
All right, how little does it all cost you then?
You were a schoolchild, now you are past middle age,
and the great drawing hasn't occurred.

I see I must be going.
I just like living,
only like living.
Sometime you must tell me of your intentions,
but now I have to stay here on this fast track
in case the provisions come along
which I won't need, being a living, breathing creature.
But I asked you about your hat.
Oh yes well it is important to have a hat.

THE LIGHTNING CONDUCTOR

The general was always particular about his withers,
lived in a newspaper tent
someone had let fall beside an easy chair.
Telling the man with no fingers what it was like to smoke a cigarette
in the Twenties, we proceeded naturally to your cousin Junius.
His plan was to overtake the now speeding tortoise
by digging some kind of a fire trench in its path,
which would cause it to wonder,
fatally, for a second,
after which we could all go back to channeling the news.
There's a story here about a kind of grass that grows in the Amazon
valley that is too tall for birds to fly over—
they fly past it instead—
yet leeches have no trouble navigating its circuitous heaps
and are wont to throw celebratory banquets afterward,
at which awards are given out—best costume in a period piece
too distracted by the rapids to notice what period it is, and so on.
Before retiring the general liked to play a game of all-white dominoes,
after which he would place his nightcap distractedly on the other man's
    crocheted chamber-pot lid.
Subsiding into fitful slumber, warily he dreams
of the giant hand descended from heaven
like the slope of a moraine, whose fingers were bedizened with rings
in which every event that had ever happened in the universe could
    sometimes be discerned.

Sometimes you end up in a slough no matter what happens,
no matter how many precautions have been taken, threads picked from the
    tapestry
that was to have provided us with underwear, and now is bare as any
grassless season, on whatever coast you choose to engage.
It's sad that many were left behind,
but a good thing for the bluebirds in their beige houses.

They never saw any reason to join the vast, confused migration,
fucking like minks as far as the spotty horizon.
It doesn't get desperately cold any more, and that's certainly a lucky
    anomaly too.

I ASKED MR. DITHERS WHETHER IT WAS TIME YET HE SAID NO TO WAIT

Time, you old miscreant! Slain any brontosauruses lately? You—
Sixty wondering days I watched him navigate the alkali lick,
always a little power ebbing, streaming from high windowsills.
Down here the tetched are lonely. There's nothing they can do
except spit.

We felt better about answering the business letter
once the resulting hubris had been grandfathered in,
slowly, by a withered sage in clogs
and a poncho vast as a delta, made of some rubbery satinlike
material. It was New Year's Eve
again. Time to get out the punch bowl,
make some resolutions,
I don't think.

HAVEN'T HEARD ANYTHING

Quietly the first hours left, amused.
We were in a quandary at first then wet our whistles
in some neighborhood bar. The throng came on strong.

It's too far off to hear the people over there,
someone said. Perhaps we should move,
another one said. Perhaps. But we were way off
and the rut in the sand only led to one place.

When the sand closes over our ease
we'll know it done.

The morose driver wept, represented his case
as somehow more urgent. Than other passengers'.
Some of them we got out.
Vanilla ice cream, I quaffed,
for it *seemed* good, for a little time at that.
The poet wanted to introduce us to his suite.
But what he really wanted to do
was play for a little time. Well, that's natural—
I mean, who among us hasn't tried?
Few, it's true, have succeeded.

Another morn he would lie in shock
over the state of poetry. "None could penetrate
the recesses of the human mind like Major Pendennis,"
he opined. We saw it coming,
or should have:
a big empty cape
on the shoulders of the oldest,
who seemed to be advancing.

He wasn't ancient, but he struck us that way.
If we'd never been to town, and heard the lights
sometime, we'd be all over a neighbor, licking,
passing out free samples of dude. But it was like
too cagey for them, none of us wanted to retire.

Since that day the memory of recognition beats
at my template. I don't know what to do with all my acquired knowledge.
I could give it to someone, I suppose. Wait, no then
they wouldn't know what to do with it.
I suppose I could be relaxed.
Yes, that's more the ticket we smiled.

CHINESE WHISPERS

And in a little while we broke under the strain:
Suppurations ad nauseam, the wanting to be taller,
though it's simply about being mysterious, i.e., not taller,
like any tree in any forest.
                              Mute, the pancake describes you.
It had tiny Roman numerals embedded in its rim.
It was a pancake clock. They had 'em in those days,
always getting smaller, which is why they finally became extinct.
It was a hundred years before anyone noticed.
                                        The governor-general
called it "sinuous." But we, we had other names for it,
knew it was going to be around for a long time,
even though extinct. And sure as shillelaghs fall from trees
onto frozen doorsteps, it came round again
when all memory of it had been expunged
                                        from the common brain.
Everybody wants to try one of those new pancake clocks.
A boyfriend in the next town had one
but conveniently forgot to bring it over each time we invited him.
Finally the rumors grew more fabulous than the real thing:
I hear they are encrusted with tangles of briar rose,
                                        so dense
not even a prince seeking the Sleeping Beauty could get inside.
What's more, there are more of them than when they were extinct,
yet the prices keep on rising. They have them in the Hesperides
and in shantytowns on the edge of the known world,
blue with cold. All downtowns used to feature them.
                                        Camera obscuras,
too, were big that year. But why is it that with so many people
who want to know what a shout is about, nobody can find the original
    recipe?
All too soon, no one cares. We go back to doing little things for each other,
pasting stamps together to form a tiny train track, and other,
less noticeable things. The past is forgotten till next time.

How to describe the years? Some were like blocks of the palest halvah,
careless of being touched. Some took each other's trash out,
put each other's eyes out. So many got thrown out
before anyone noticed, it was like a chiaroscuro

                                    of collapsing clouds.
How I longed to visit you again in that old house! But you were deaf,
or dead. Our letters crossed. A motorboat was ferrying me out past
the reef, people on shore looked like dolls fingering stuffs.

                                                      More
keeps coming out about the dogs. Surely a simple embrace
from an itinerant fish would have been spurned at certain periods. Not
    now.
There's a famine of years in the land, the women are beautiful,
but prematurely old and worn. It doesn't get better. Rocks half-buried
in bands of sand, and spontaneous execrations.

                                    I yell to the ship's front door,
wanting to be taller, and somewhere in the middle all this gets lost.
I was a phantom for a day. My friends carried me around with them.

It always turns out that much is salvageable.

                                    Chicken coops
haven't floated away on the flood. Lacemakers are back in business
with a vengeance. All the locksmiths had left town during the night.
It happened to be a beautiful time of season, spring or fall,
the air was digestible, the fish tied in love knots
on their gurneys. Yes, and journeys

were palpable too: Someone had spoken of saving appearances
and the walls were just a little too blue in mid-morning.
Was there ever such a time? I'd like to handle you,
bruise you with kisses for it, yet something always stops me short:
the knowledge that this isn't history,

                                    no matter how many
times we keep mistaking it for the present, that headlines

trumpet each day. But behind the unsightly school building, now a pickle
warehouse, the true nature of things is known, is not overridden:
Yours is a vote like any other. And there is fraud at the ballot boxes,
stuffed with lace valentines and fortunes from automatic scales,
dispensed with a lofty kind of charity, as though this could matter
to us, these tunes
                    carried by the wind
from a barrel organ several leagues away. No, this is not the time
to reveal your deception to us. Wait till rain and old age
have softened us up a little more.
                                    Then we'll see how extinct
the various races have become, how the years stand up
to their descriptions, no matter how misleading,
and how long the disbanded armies stay around. I must congratulate you
on your detective work, for I am a connoisseur
of close embroidery, though I don't have a diploma to show for it.

The trees, the barren trees, have been described more than once.
Always they are taller, it seems, and the river passes them
without noticing. We, too, are taller,
our ceilings higher, our walls more tinctured
with telling frescoes, our dooryards both airier and vaguer,
according as time passes and weaves its minute deceptions in and out,
a secret thread.
Peace is a full stop.
And though we had some chance of slipping past the blockade,
now only time will consent to have anything to do with us,
for what purposes we do not know.

IN THE TIME OF PUSSY WILLOWS

This is going to take some time.
Nope, it's almost over. For today anyway.
We'll have a beautiful story, old story
to fish for as his gasps come undone.

I never dreamed the pond of chagrin
would affect me this much. Look, I'm shaking,
shrinking with the devil
in the stagy sunrise he devised.
Then there will be no letters for what is truth,
to make up the words of it. It will be standing still
for all it's worth. A hireling shepherd came along,
whistling, his eyes on the trees. He was a servant of two masters,
which is some excuse, although not really all that much of a one.
Anyway, he overstayed his welcome. The last train had already left.

How does one conduct one's life amid such circumstances,
dear snake, who want the best for us
as long as you're not hurt by it?
My goodness, I thought I'd seen a whole lot of generations,
but they are endless, one keeps following another,
treading on its train, hissing.

What a beautiful old story it could be after all
if those in the back rows would stop giggling for a minute.
By day, we paddled and arbitraged
to get to this spot. By night it hardly matters.
Strange we didn't anticipate this,
but the dumbest clues get overlooked by the smartest gumshoe
and we're back in some fetishist's vinyl paradise
with no clue as to how we got here
except the tiny diamond on your pillow—it must have been a tear
hatched from a dream, when you actually knew what you were doing.
Now, it's all fear. Fear and wrongdoing.

Our outboard motor sputters and quits, and silence
beats down from every point in the sky. To have digested this
when we were younger, and felt a set of balls coming on . . .
It may be that thunder and lightning are two-dimensional,
that there was never really any place for fear,
that others get trapped, same as us, and make up
amusing stories to cover their tracks. Wait,
there's one in the donjon wants to speak his piece. Rats,
now he's gone too.

Yes, he slipped and died in front of you,
and you intend to twist this into an ethos?
Go make up other stories.
Window reflected in the bubble,
how often I've tried to pray to you,
but your sphere would have nothing of it.
I felt almost jinxed. Then a spider led the way
back into the room

and I knew why we'd never left. Outside was brushfires.
Here was the peace of Philemon and Baucis,
offering chunks of bread and salami to the tattered stranger,
and a beaker of wine darker than the deepest twilight,
a table spread with singularities
for the desperate and tragic among us.

Angel, come back please. Let us smell your heavenly smell again.

THE AMERICAN

It's dull, no realism. A no-color. To what
formlessness have we committed? How fond I am
of it blew off the pensive boarder
hunkered amid lilacs, a hoverer, as meat loves salt.
Such scenes are not uncommon in this
world of decent gin, this midden whose ungodly
stench plunders all inserts of a keepable diary.

Why call them stones?
Swapping and cheating are as a labor of love
for all concerned. I try to read some sense
into the minutes but am usually rebuffed,
as scorched linen yells at the ironing board's
grace note of intrigue. Sooner or later
we send them packing, and they leave us—it's
so simple? Don't you love it? Ask later whether
we and they were loved. Someone should know. In 150, 160 years
they'll be beholden, you can bet. And not knowing what
those others want has all along been a jiffy.
The shelf's canceled

from the Adriatic to the Antarctic, my footsteps cast
incredibly long shadows, though that's not for you to macerate.
Or masticate. I who matriculated was perhaps
meant to be a lover unto you
through the unabated storm's portholes—dear, we're
here because he asked us to wait some more.

THE SEVENTIES

For a long time things seemed to go astutely.
Every evening at four the unspooling showed us
its friendly face. "I will treat you well,
on my honor." In those days, no one kept records
or took notice of things much. It was
possible to live as an entity.

Still, surprising things were overheard
from time to time. Voices that seemed to come from a garage
with a third option no one had been told about.

Something about a shipwreck. It was probably OK.

We began to grow impatient
about peace and war, after a busy day of relaxation
few around us could contain or apprehend.
The money fish had been strapped to my thigh.
Otherwise I might have turned informant, living out my days
in a Tudor bungalow under the witness protection program.
I needed the cash. The rest was just net profit and loss.

ALL THAT NOW

How old? The fish and the lake
swam around together, easily bored.
The belly of a courtier leans forth.
It is mild weather. Just so much we know.

So much we know and cannot have it
in our little hands. The mouse goes to bed.
A neighbor is placing his false teeth
in a glass of water. You say, not like this,

like this, but too much wells up—
the patient outline of the maples' faces,
the brook that ran too far,
into some intelligence or other.

Amber and vanilla are all what we know,
how can it be so? Whose little tootsie
are you, once? Did the elephant
walk silently past your house, one

night when you were out?
None of the children escapes—
dam, waterfall, how could we hear
it in the crashing noise? Whose complaint

goes unregistered? How many of us are there,
anyway? Or were, some, some of the time.
Mayhap in dreams
a lady kisses a far shuttle,

warning away visions of Kansas
and outer suburbia, where cows work.
You came back from that dung
as from another world,

one that made you and broke you
four times in the course of your life.
Yet, you were "splendid."
You have answered every question.

TRUTH GLEAMS

"I threw a hairnet over the dry cleaner's embroidery. It wasn't long before something shot out of the rain pipe, between my ankles. An animus avoided me. The surface was fractured. Why do you come here, old man? Leave your nosegay of nettles on the altar in the side street. We don't want too much of any one thing today. But you and your dog can stay."

"Nor will I know what to eat, when she rounds the curve of bananas. The altar offered little but idle chitchat. How far you've come if it's autumn, and the plagues will surround you nervously, waiting for an opening. It could be anything, or just about anything, it seems. I am nervous with waiting in this alley of darkened peanut vendors. Mayhap some will come to inquire about me. After all, I was on your board of regents, too, when I was young. Maybe this may not be made to count. I offer you affection, distilled from the worldly tisanes of the stranger who stalked us here, once, offering insurance."

"I can go no further. In the dark is drama and I am the better for it, though I have skimmed . . . When the Bakerloo line takes over there will be loud crumpling as of wrapping paper, and those hens won't know us, will become effective barring Saturday night. If only sandpaper were all . . ."

"Listen, I have a riddle for you. What swings and stands in place? Now you are not to answer if you know, leaving the sacrificial stone for other, younger—my heavens! Can it be? We stayed up three nights, purposely depriving ourselves of sleep in the interests of a greater god-fiction. Now I seem to see these mules in the afterglow, coming down the side of the mountain, their saddlebags packed with sapphires from the monarch's glen. Truly the cows have escaped, the cock has risen, paying respects to all that gleams regardless. And the nearest is best after all. Like a perfumed armpit, thoughts take root and break off, and it is not so much the absence of an almanac but the presence of modern history books that testifies to our sudden chagrin, bound in red and olive, their gold lettering sputtering through the tides. Marry, if it was me I'd tell them the truth just for once, to be off on it. And their sable sides yield nothing, no rebuke, not even a reflection, for once in a way."

"Aye but if it was you you'd do it differently."

"Aye and that I would, but folks'd know why it was me and why. The tentative chains that stimulate can't make a young mother happy, her tears are too green for that, yet if sometime somebody could come up with an effective mooring, who knows how wide of us we'd end up? Like a shower of rosewater on a difficult day. Then we all come out to play in the garbage, and the sense of nothing is no more. Checkmate! I've baffled you, hasn't it? Here, take this caramel, it's little enough for what you and the sand are worth. And every day the tide shifts a little to the east, reconfiguring the shore. I could get what I want at last if I needed it."

"My shirt is off to you, I'll bleed through three blizzards ere we come to a crossways not of my own pullulating, but that's just how you got off and what it takes, stiff. No more mayflies for the convention. Meanwhile you can be sure *someone's* watching, someone wants ever so much to join our stitchery be it cloven, yet it is glued to one side, they pass through unseeing, the tide's out, the night too. Anybody wants some of these can take 'em. Babes who've seen too much, underscored by the petunia blight that crept over the last two decades of the century that recently ended, as far as the 'I' can see. Coffee?"

LITTLE SICK POEM

If living is a hate crime, so be it.
But hey—I was around when they invented the Cardiff giant.
I kid you not. God wanted you to know,
so you'd remember to love Him. Yes, He often confides in me,

tips me off to the whereabouts of valuable junk
but doesn't want me to let on we are in cahoots.
This lamp, covered in rust, is valuable
though not old. It is collectible,
as we all are, in a sense. I love you,
it's sexual harassment, but we get on that way,
through bluster, through dried open fields.

If I were you I'd get an unlisted number,
then think about growing up, just a little.
I can't tell you which divining bones to choose, that's your job,
and when you come close, I wish it was all around,

around over me. The jingle of your hat comforts me,
confirms me in my worst aspects. I shall never be anything but a clown,
now. And there's so much work to do,
so many puzzles to ignore.

A MAN CLAMORED

That strike ended and another one began.
None of them were long. One further loop.
In the olive valleys they live
the way we did a hundred years ago.
Speculation stems from a fissure
in the valley's steep side.
There is no room for bathing
any more in that. She saw us
make eye contact.

The police, a few of them, are years old.
It was a nice beginning for a story
that might never end, so we chose a more careful
one instead. It's free fall in the trees now.
Twilight is a firm maybe. The cobbler's
children wear shoes to school, even in the rain.
Perhaps it's time for them and us.
You wore a yellow dress and selected earrings.

LOCAL LEGEND

Arriving late at the opera one night
I ran into Dr. Gradus ad Parnassum hastening down the marble stair,
swan-like. "I wouldn't bother if I was you," he confided.
"It's a Verdi work written before he was born.
True, his version of the Faust legend is unique:
Faust tempts Mephistopheles to come up with something
besides the same old shit. Finally, at his wit's end, the devil
urges Valentine to take his place, promising him big rewards
this side of Old Smoky. Then, wouldn't you know, Gretchen gets involved.
They decide to make it into a harassment case. No sooner
does Faust hit the street than the breeze waffles his brow,
he can't say where he came from, or if he ever had a youth
to be tempted back into."
                                        The bats arrived. It was their moment.
Twenty million bats fly out of an astonishingly low culvert
every night, in season. I kid you not. After a cursory swoop
or two, they all fly back in. It all happens in a matter of
minutes, seconds, almost. Which reminds me, have you chosen your
        second?
Mephisto wants you to use this foil. It works better.
No, there's nothing wrong with it.

Hours later I stood with the good doctor
in a snow-encrusted orchard. He urged the value
of mustard plasters on me. "See, it makes sense."
Yet we both knew they are poisonous in some climates,
though only if taken in minute quantities.

See you again, old thing.

MEET ME TONIGHT IN DREAMLAND

It was an hour ago. I walked upstairs to dreamland. Took a cab and got out
and somebody else backed in. Now we weren't actually on the Dreamland
floor. That would be for later. Look, these are the proper plans, plants.
They used to have a Chautauqua here, far out into the lake. Now it's
peeled. No one actually comes here. Yet there are people. You just hardly
ever see them. No I wasn't being modest. Some get out on the floor, several
a year, whose purple glass sheds an eldritch glow on the trottoirs, as
Whitman called them. Or spittoons. Look, we are almost a half a mile
later, it must link up. The Tennessee drifter smiled sharkly. Then it was on
to native board games.

Je bois trop.

In one of these, called "Skunk," you are a weasel chasing a leveret back
to its hole when Bop! the mother weasel, about ten stories tall, traps you
with her apron string, patterned with poppies and rotted docks. You see,
you thought every noun had to have an adjective, even "sperm," and that's
where you made your first big mistake. Later it's raining and we have to
take a car. But the game isn't over—there are sixteen thousand marble
steps coming up, down which you glide as effortlessly as you please, as
though on a bicycle, weasel in tow. It's an exercise bike. What a time to
tell me, the solar wind has sandpapered everything as smooth as quartz.
Now it's back to the finish line with you.

You're not quite out of the woods yet. Dreamland has other pastures, other
melodies to chew on. Hummingbirds mate with dragonflies beneath the
broken dome of the air, and it's three o'clock, the sun is raining mineral-
colored candy. I'd like one of these. It's yours. Now I'm glad we came. I
hate drafts though and the sun is slowly moving away. I'm standing on the
poop deck wiggling colored pennants at the coal-colored iceberg that
seems to be curious about us, is sliding this way and that, then turns
abruptly back into the moors with their correct hills in the distance. If it
was me I'd take a trip like this every day of my life.

ORNERY FISH

Wind your way to the floor,
sweet. No passions obtain today.
We are full of vinaigrette,
cursed by the rain for being rained on.

This pass has expired.
I thought we had retreated
until I noticed you far out in the field,
waving a crimson handkerchief

toward someone I couldn't see.
This is the way it goes: I
come back, then you come back to me.
Our heads blend in the twilight tea.

Once, we thought it was over.
A man claimed to be giving away
all he had. Actually he kept much of it.
Now, he can't give it away,

or get arrested in Utica. The violence
of which I was so important a part
is chiefly lilacs now—purple,
speedy shelter. Toward you it climbs

like a ladder in the wall
of a besieged city. Trouble is, the city
has already fallen, the starved inhabitants
are welcoming us invaders with streamers;

there is a pit where the golf course was
but milk supplies are normal
again. From the towers of the frescoed fun house
the virgins are beseeching: let it all happen

again, let this come over us,
travel over us like a wave or time,
from which protrudes a tiny fist
clutching orange or yellow flowers.

PORTRAIT WITH A GOAT

We were reading to ourselves. Sometimes to others.
I was quietly reading the margin
when the doves fell, it was blue
outside. Perhaps in a moment,
he said. The moment never came.
I was reading something else now,
it didn't matter. Other people came and
dropped off their résumés. I wasn't being idle,
exactly. Someone wanted to go away
altogether in this preposterous season.

THE DECALS IN THE HALLWAY

remanded Margery to an earlier contingency:
Sir Isaac fishing for compliments
in troubled waters, and like that. In a flash, a star
o'erspread their terrestrial inhibitions. Mother's
hairnet came unknotted. She dabbled in bliss
all her life, early knew perfection's spiteful sting.

He'd imbibed his father-in-law's authority
as though it were ichor. Sometimes, transplanted
to the elephant's-foot umbrella stand
in the vestibule, he'd curse children and the impossible
trail of conundrums they leave behind. It'd
be just like him, she thought, to leave
on the eve of the midnight of their secrecy,
secretly planning to be around next morning
when the gulls had drifted away and the engines given
out.

And sweet it was to contemplate the immediate
future of immediacy. Iris and the little ones had run out onto the street,
cries came from the corner, like dishes falling
absentmindedly against each other.
Another corker, she planned. Instead
the call went out: Diversify! And in so doing
casually assuage some of your dopiest penchants. Here,
the anesthetized markets of the world await,
prostrate, time's scalpel's hobson-jobson,
while ninnies panic under the pancake tree, touting wired panaceas,
spillovers of earlier attractions, tie-in deals
with the Old One himself.

Cool invitations now apply.
Every faction would like to own its kind of behavior,
though we weren't being modern just then. Far from it:

We were thinking money shots in Piazzola plazas
of retching grief, where not one codicil reaches striplinghood
unsieved. Yet the hole that encounters a crater
knows which antidote to swallow. Lord Henry waded far out
into the crabs' private estuary, yet the water never grazed his knees.
The sun-driven sky's paisley was as good as perjured; as collateral
it had probably peaked; yet who precisely are these camp followers,
and what is it that they think we have done that they want to ask us about?

As one protuberant pubescent I was tossed, over and over again in a
    blanket.
Sometimes I think I live there still. Certain declivities interested me then,
made me think about grad school, if only
to get away from the archaic rumblings.
I'd face an Everest of chilblains just to insinuate myself
with the wolf, one more time. They told us he was out, not to wait.
The joke was on them, they said.
They'll be back soon.

ECHOLALIA RAG

1.
The garage door is unlocked. Your
"tantalizing fragrance" roars over me
like a word.
What word?
Well I wasn't going to utter that,
not today. It's too late.
For today, it's late.

We can take the train back tomorrow.
There's still time to catch the last one.

The sun was still high in the heavens—

2.
My gawd all the chickens
in whatever coop
riding high,
heading our way,
another legend, palpably untrue, but which will be around for a long time.

Human error caused a collision
of houndstooth check and puffs
of train smoke

and apple blossoms.
Here are blossoms for you—
you know, "habitat,"
and what to put into it
now.

3.
When the gingerbread boy
did his morose errand
it was melting on the ground,
felt tubing on the floor,
like a good scare
isn't around anymore,
like even you knew it
coming on in your car, the sun,
melted cheese over whiskey down:
Don't sneeze yet.

THE EVENING OF GREUZE

As a group we were somewhat vulnerable
and are so today. My brother-in-law has fixed
me a tower in the mill, from whose oriel
I can see the bluebottles who nag heaven
with their unimportance. But what are they expected to do?
Raise families? Become deacons? If so my calculations
collapse into bric-a-brac, my equations
are undone.

Across the road they are building a cement house.
It will seemingly have no windows. A columbarium
for cement pigeons. And ever as I talked to you
down the decades in my letters one thing was unsure:
your reply. Now we are again endangered,
like dead birds, and autumn's ruby spittle mounts
in the sky like a tornado. Try to keep
cold and empty in this bare room.
Examine mirrors in the studio.
The lizard's glint, the horse's velvet blanket
will surprise you into veiled hope one day.

AS UMBRELLAS FOLLOW RAIN

Too bad he never tried it—
he might have liked it.

She saw us make eye contact.
And that was that for that day.

Too bad he too, when I
am

meaning if I came along it'd
already be too late.

Some of the swans are swarming.
The spring has gone under—it wasn't
supposed to be like this.

Now they watch him and cringe.
Who are they? Who is he?

We decided to fly Chinese.
The food wasn't that good.

And oh Erwin did I tell you
that man—the one—I didn't

know if I was supposed to or not.
He crawled back listlessly,

holding a bunch of divas.
It's hard work getting these out,

but so's any thing you're entitled to do:
classes to attend.

The morning of school.
Evening almost over,

they bend the security rules.
It's time for another fog bomb.

Lookit the way they all roost.
Poor souls clashed together

until almost the root's roof
separates us from our beginning.

We slew many giants in our day,
burned many libraries.

Roundabouts, swings,
it was all one piece of luck to us.

Now we're washed up it's almost cold.
Not bad enough to put up a stand.

Out of that longing we built a paean.
Now everyone who crosses this bridge is wiser.

It doesn't tilt much.
Look, the shore is arriving laterally.

Some people literally think they know a lot,
gets 'em in trouble, we must rake out

cafés looking for rats and exploded babies.
There was one too many last week.

I don't know if you're coding.
The cop pulled us over

in a shawl. Why do you want to go around me
when there are other circulars

to be had for the looking?
I never thought about being grounded forever.

This is Mademoiselle. Take your hat off.
There's no need, I was here last Thursday.

All the best creatures are thwarted
for their pains. He removed my chains deftly,

processed my passport with gunk.
Now two times five geese fly across

the crescent moon, it is time to get down to
facts, in the tiny park.

There were priests posing as nuns,
quinces and stuff.

Tilt me a little more to the sun,
I want to see it one last time. There,

that's just fine. I've seen it.
You can roll me inside. On wings of what perturbation?

He came for the julep.
He was gone in an instant.

We cry too much over
drowned dogs.

He came in last week too.
Said he knew you or somebody else.

It's the pain just of replying
that makes so many of them take up different lines.

Too many goods—we are spoiled indeed.
Had we learned to subsist on less

the changing of the world might be different,
earth come to greet us. I say, the chairs have grown back.

The couple sat in the dish drainer
pondering an uncertain future.

The kitchen had never looked bleaker
except for two chinchillas near the stove, a beaker

of mulled claret, shaving soap smelling
so fresh and new, like smoke, almost.

He says leave it here,
that he comes here.

OK harness the DeSoto,
we'll have other plans

for newness, for a renewing, kind of—
picnics in the individual cells

so no one falls asleep for it, dreams
she is a viola, instrument of care, of sorts.

You should have seen him when we got back.
He was absolutely wild. Hadn't wanted us to go

to the picture show. But in a way it was all over,
we were back, the harm had been done.

Gradually he came to realize this
over a period of many years, spanning

two world wars and a major depression.
After that it was time to get up and go,

but who had the get up and go? A child's
party, painted paper hats, bowlfuls of lemonade,

no more at the lemonade stand, it sold out.
That was cheerful. A man came right up behind you,

he had two tickets to the door.
We need starve no more

but religion is elastic too—
might want some at some future date—

if so you'll find it here.
We have to hurry in now,

hurry away, it's the same thing
she said as rain came and stole the king.

UNDER CELLOPHANE

None of it helped much,
not even my beloved Philosophy,
sitting dejected, hands in her lap,
moving her head slowly from side to side.
"You naughty, wicked boy . . ."

But I cherished you last night . . .
It makes no difference, night is like that—
different, odd. The gains we rack up
dissipate in cold daylight, random
to the touch. Look how the faint green
of the willow shudders. Last night it was another story,
some kind of bird was singing.
I have this warble in my head
yet can't get out of my long johns . . .

And if it was over, from side to side, rocking
as a distraught mother rocks her cradle
mindless of the screaming babe,
and if it all comes to this, what good are we to others
when we do descend the stair?
Lamplight and this and that, caring
out of one end of the tube, with the other hand
fastening the necklace clasp—
Oh you had some fine times too,
morning like pasteboard reflecting the light
at the dancing houses, and
a world wondering, opening like a bud.

You remember I was locked in a closet
and when someone came to let me out,
said, what is this lovely garden,
but where is the even lovelier one I was just in?
So all things come to bust:

the Joshua trees piling ever higher
their grief under the conservatory's blank panes,
the way you look tonight,
the way you spun your tires
in the wet gutter, on gravel, in the sand.

And take this last piece of medicine:
You were found with the rest of your litter
dying or dead. Only you showed
some appropriate curiosity
that's gone now to fan the flames
of scholarly ethics, and that's just about all we're about.

REMINISCENCES OF NORMA

Knowledgeably, she is knowledgeable about many things—
the stars in their errant orbits, a bud
sliding over a hibiscus, a cloud like a frown
on the face of a teddy bear. And then, more stuff.
The inquisitors were endlessly patient, amused—
you had to be, in that business.
And if they liked your answer, you were free.
It didn't have to be true. Streamers, party favors,
confetti—all were yours.
I know now why some have seen the sun sink
and it fed their hunger, they came on unabated.
Is it my lord's pleasure to mate?
In that case we have pogo sticks of different sizes and colors.
But he may just go away
thinking it enough for that day.

Bicycle came barreling through the sleet—

OBSIDIAN HOUSE

> The fruits are ripe, dipped in fire, cooked
> and tested here on earth.
> —Hölderlin, translated by Richard Sieburth

as was proven
when they entered the house
in which the priest was,
moping and sincere

like all exegetes. Zeppelin
hovered o'er him, bushes fancied him,
but it was to be let down on earth
they all embraced singing.

Further, one was sure
one had come to pass,
yet no slovenly proof was
ever forwarded.

The lines swayed
backwards and forth,
housewives queuing up for lamb chops
and all that this rhythm implies

excoriated
from above.

The tourist metastasizes his position.
These palms are lucky being within us
no matter what the tyrant truth says.
All along my childhood's wall

I hoped (was hoping) for this occlusion
but not passionately.
A cheerful emotion hatched,
soon population o'erran the land.

We descended gently toward boats
to hear the boatswain's
song, sung from the capstan, about how life intrudes
on the plodding waves

and no one is certain of desiccation
as a great marrow bone is gnawed.
It is as though a feast had happened
in plain sight. We forgot about the
treasure, forgot it had happened
among the madness of whirling wheat.

OH EVENINGS

The man standing there, the other stranger,
slips easily into the background
as though stopping were the last thing on his mind.

Another, lacking the courage of his convictions,
went mad from drinking seawater. That was an absolute rout.

Oh evenings! Learning where to look it up
became an end in itself. To this purpose
trained fleas were engaged to do sums.
Ants on their way to happiness paused
over the numbers: Did it seem like three
or was it just three? Is this where I came in?

More likely we all need to be blessed for the hole
in his savage argument. Surely, passing through town,
we contributed a little to the regional economy,
received credit for showing our faces.
So what if the only theater in town
had been turned into a funeral parlor?
There are few things more theatrical than death,
one supposes, though one doesn't know.

Which brings me to my original argument.
Ah, what was the argument? Keeping our places,
assuming no more credit than what is due
our tame luster, our positive shine. Then people will go out
into the city, spreading germs, living like it was last year.

INTRICATE FASTING

This little bridge
three of them
blasted a recess in the rock
hoovered the mountains
played with a squirrel called Scrawny
(hangnail on the forefinger of Death)
a hundred yards from my home
what home you haven't got a home
I do so have a home

Mottled later the pattern recedes
into my marvelous life
Hey how are you life
never been better
that's good
'cause I want you to take care of yourself
understand
Yeah I understand
Aw for the love of Pete
The pattern's got on mushrooms now
on the clothes of aborigines on magnets
They are sending a boat for you a
private launch

Tired of feeding the muskrats in this shithole
getting ready to tidy up and go
leave this wooden structure that doesn't love me
Wait there are one or two small items to regulate
before you can go
I repeat I want my life out of here
dissolved in memory
Bring on the aromatherapy
boys there's a job to get done

Me always in the middle
me whining
me probably not such a nice person after all
me on the stadium
me persiflating in the dire blue strait
me up to my ankles in woe
me rejoicing in the realization of my perfectibility

Loggerheads come on down
They're waiting for you
in the cabin
this way please,

And that should be about right—

ALONE, I

know *of* him. I don't want
to speak of him. He's brilliant.
His underwear is radiant.
The Davis Cup
came apart in his hands. A seasoned jester.
A basket case. Mother brought the children.
We all survived tennis.
The gale picked up.

Buildings waved in it, and the tentacles
of a giant squid, seeking a memento
lost some years ago near the Donner Pass.
Seriously, I want my memento back!
The cabin cruisers of morning
edge tentatively closer—
why, it's all a sham!
Prince Charming's dropping cigarette ash
on topiary chessmen. The ugly sisters are uncertain.
Cinderella is out. Period. Gargoyles are in great demand,
but if so, why say so? You'll come back, with childhood lusting
after evil groceries, and more of them to take care of.
Youth is wasted on the old.
Like I said, the days, these days, come calibrated.

WINTER DAYDREAMS

On the boulevard I passed a giant squid.
It manifested but a puny interest in me
or its surroundings, though one suction cup
thoughtfully grazed a ring of spikes around a boulevard tree
like a monocle one puts down absentmindedly
on the page of a newspaper and words like
worker ants quickly spring into action:
"It was not the FIRST TIME THE accused has been so solicited.
By his OWN ADMISsion four other rumpuses were given rise to
after that first YEar . . ."

I was almost home then, by subterfuge or sheer pluck.
In the underbrush a walrus crows,
all decency shed, or shredded.
Little wonder that home is a bright place to be
if living's your thing.

RUNWAY

We crawled out of the car
into the rest stop. Lady Baltimore cake
was served by Madame du Barry look-alikes.
"Don't hurry, Mr. Executioner," one chirped,
pressing the unwanted crumbs against my lips.
"It'll all be over in a second," she added encouragingly.

Red Skelton asked me if I had a book coming out. He seemed drowned
in lists of trivia and itching-powder dreams—
the kind that make you wake up
and then sort of fall back into sleep again.
His brother was cleaning up after the elephants. He
wore a crisp white uniform. Could have been a soda jerk,
or just a jerk. My scented glove offends
the daintiest among them, for they have no recourse
but cries of old London—an exhaustive repertory,
one first thought, but soon its coda reared—
a clutch of mordant shrieks.

I supposed it was the witching hour.
Nothing unusual happened. Soon we were leaving home
forever, to be pitched about on storm-tossed seas,
flagrant to be back amid multiple directions. For though there are some
who can live without compasses, it dissolves all complexity
if one is perpetually in the know. Sleep, directions—that's all
I need at my chaste fireside, to take in the sights,
just as the wind starts and darkness longs
to take us down a peg.

RANDOM JOTTINGS OF AN OLD MAN

Like a fool, I let him into my house,
and he began dropping jottings everywhere.
Where once crepe-paper flowers had been,
jottings overflowed the basin into the water closet.

Urban affairs had kept him—
something about a rendezvous with kelp. "Hurry,
the paths of nature are creeping
to the corrugated tooth. And it's a blitz of old stars,
tonight!" Something in me leaned into the vacant doorframe.
It was a still life of bottles and a jar
that once had held cold cream. We mustn't wait here
for him, that's what he wants, and
if we do so he'll want to eat us.

No more us to be with in the morning,
among the cups and shards. No more sticky places on the railing.
We held hands there too, once, for years, watching the
palms move out into the harbor.
The pianola never recovered from the loss.

Today the air is bright again and fresh with pods.
No mourners were sighted on the post road.
He came down to us with relaxed meaning in his grin,
cudgeled, cajoled us, told us breezy stories
about a widow in the henhouse.

After all regrets have been pocketed, the counter wiped clean
of terrible fingerprints, assuredly one moves westward
into sheepherding country. The ranchers won't like it,
but they'll let us live, closer to dying
than many insects are now, attracted by the chiming and gleams of the
    cash register.

Other oaths, other options will follow
in the wake of spring.

Millions of mullions waken, gesticulate to us.

HER CARDBOARD LOVER

The way you look tonight
is perishable, unphotographable, laughable. Sometimes
dyslexia strikes in late middle age. You are
the way I look tonight. *At last
my love has come along.*
And you are mine at last.
Slowly the orchestra wives pick over the set,
go behind a wall. The big smiley man is thinking,
thinking he has an IDEA! Well, if he says so.
You gotta believe him. One orchestra wife comes back.
She has forgotten her pearls. The orchestra riffs around,
they come back. "Well, I never! Of all things!"
Oh, it plays

to the breach. You see it. Her lover and best friend came
along the hall. "I'm sorry, Dan.
But I just couldn't." So it's all alright,
he thinks. He thinks it's a secret.

MOON, MOON

The winter voice adjusts: "As I was saying
(before I was so rudely interrupted),
we don't have to go downstairs and get the plants.
Some of them, at least, are already here."

More innocent people, gnawed by pests.
Death agreed to lie low for a while.
Nobody was very grateful. "After all,
if it hadn't been for him the anteaters
might have noticed us. Now potstickers take up
the cry: 'It was great to have you in that glen!' "

Out on the ice children are being sick
as grown men whirl round and round
the devil in coattails. "He had a passion for straw marquetry.
Other than that, little is known
of him or of his descendants."

In the valley of the school all is well anew.
"I told you all would be well
on a certain day." That rivulets
would course past their snowy banks, singing the song of
a sudden thaw in January.

"Each of us checked out the others,
got down to work." His disguise worked,
he made it through the breadline with blue
Etruscan flowers in his galvanized wrists:

"It is time for the debit to begin,
the rush of evening." "No one likes being abandoned
on a rapidly disintegrating floe, and dawn coming."
He stood just outside.

We were the undeserving ones now, though his warmth
cradles us,
as the road becomes a kiss.

SYLLABUS

Look,
the savage glitter of downtown,
those walls of glycerin
inspissated by tears—
yes, and why does the smell not go away?
Honey, it's been ages, take off your hat and coat,
rest your feet awhile? Now, where were we?

Wave upon wave of new construction
(some of it shoddy), then that too plowed under
as new waves bare their teeth—
where's it gotten us? I say, you
look a little disheveled—want to freshen up?
Play doctor? Uh, I'll be with you
in a moment. Yes, the doctor is in,
yuk yuk. Now, what was it we were learning to say?

"Change the value systems. All incandescence and fear
have their origin there. In not nice night
one must strip down silently, and quickly.
See, a little headway has been made."

The snow shovel's disclaimer
defused the situation. Soon the host was ruddy
with his own reflected good cheer.
And it was again time to creep back a ways,
to rest, sheltered by soffits,
and pronounce one's own alphabet, nasally and distinctly, backwards
like it was supposed to be all along. We'd arrived
again, it seemed, though we only came along for the ride.

ON HIS RELUCTANCE TO TAKE DOWN
THE CHRISTMAS ORNAMENTS

A nice, normal morning:
feet setting out as though in a trance,
doubling the yesterdays, a doubled man
under the stairs, and strange surrealist fish
from so much disappearance, damaged in the mail.

Or the spry cutting edge of another day.
Here, we have these in
sizes and colors—
day goes fluttering by.

Like ivy behind a chimney
it grows and grows in ropes.
Mouse teams unslay it,
yeomen can't hear yet.

A shadow purling,
up into the sky.
Silence in the vandalized vomitorium.

It's great that you can be here too.
Passivity rests its case.

THE BUSINESS OF FALLING ASLEEP

Set this down too:
That one who was cognizant
(belief in one to three things)
turned at last to the roulette table
and gasped her last—or else, why not let the building sleep
while it collapses, spineless. In a second
the faith that was as large as my life was split,
edge to edge—

And tell them this:
If it was for nothing that I aged in a dawdle
beside a slow-knocking stream
out from under the reader,
why am I being criticized?
Do you react to fine breath of the anvil
in a cold room?
More, then, another time—but we will have to
fit note to note,
unclenchingly
going over more territory until it all rises
smooth from the gulf,
a pure provocation,
arc of seamless energy.

The wall-bearing fragments move on over
the main chancel.
All the tesserae fly apart.
Bracts are fresh and new.

In the main parlor the governor
seated around his table, smilingly assented
to whatever assignment was raised.
Pawky, canny—not one of your average sterns
fitted against the exodus

out of old harbors and disks in chains—
Say they came to see you,
now is calm, and whatever remaining communicants leased your
indoor policy.

Amazing, to amaze,
falling light over and in on its own imperfect
sense of the appropriate,
the main argument emerges:
how to be understand please, not with
a harpsichord at one's traces—
the dreams only pool off again, that way.
Other firm magnets enticed
girls out in summer night
where a pale loggia echoed. The neighbors fell silent,
or it was not a day in which to have elicited model policy demeanors.

HINTS AND FRAGMENTS

The arty set adheres
to the stolen pavement. Inside
are sherbets and "Barbara."
Strange, how one day

you'll come over "all queer,"
then next day we're scrambling to stamp it out.
Such are our inspirations:
of unequal value, one chasing the better
ones until he stops, forgetting. That's

the time I like best, cold color of cistern.
Values show up in the neighborhood house;
next day it's moved on.

In the Pennsylvania of my youth, tungsten filaments
daubed hoardings ludicrous shades, one after another.
The crowds have bicycled far out to see you fail.
Don't disappoint them.

Three on a match he said
is how it all began. Seven years' bad luck
and after that, roseate perspectives garlanded
with octaves of blooms. Keeping next to her
and the door closes, kindly.

All that's behind us, or
so we used to say.
Kettle's on the hob, ghost dancers
are fierce tonight. Yet it collects
in the hollow of my palm, somehow,
tears in an appetizing equation.

Door is shut,
but hasn't been locked yet.
We owe this to our childhood dogs,
sprig of hope. Where clarity once ruled
dreams are still active,
a clarinet floats ashore,
a good time was had by all.

IF YOU ASK ME

The whole is stasis between ends. Probability's dark inching, sundered,
disclaimer. Time for the space hut to close. Petal on a chain.

Thus it was the laborious leopard pirated more than one freedom hymn.
Kettle boils, not urgent.

Privately there were interviews the sun of the sea drowned. In that chair.
Over there.

When I last got a message from him I was too ill to see, into the hole,
an enchantment. Privately, then a scale. Turnips aboard, the sport tank
is partially invaded by flying fish. One youth seriously injured, two more
in critical but stable condition.

I see. It flies down to that. Why couldn't you have asked, then advised me?
Now wherever I go it'll always be a tiny tricycle behind me, stifled prunes,
prurience of a moment seen through the loupe. Best to cash everything in,
a train approaches on the narrowing rails, veering sideways. An untidy
philosopher tosses it aside like bones. Then the water rose slightly,

underground. Dare I say the water table? There will be no élan, as in a peach,
miles away, stiffening. You can say it how you like it. Screws up in
no time. The Dixie Adder is programmed livid. It likes to stop. You too.
You too in canvas bearing supple testimony away, do the lanterns recognize
terror in our faces, condition of gone, perhaps further, more than you know.
I gave him what there was to give. At the end it was invisible. It was a lot.

THE HAVES

Many there were that.
There were many who that.
Many did that to what.
Many undid that to what.
Many there were worse than that.
To undo that many did that.
More of an obstacle to this than that
where the upcoming is done to that.

The undone is done is that.
They are speaking to what is done
not left on the stove.
The done is that to that done.

There were many who did this and that,
meanwhile were many who undid that.
The undone undid the that.
The crisis under the batter's hat.

Do you manage a common if?
If so why is the crisis that?
Who did the crisis there?
Why is the crisis after my time that.

Ordinarily men go around
seeking wedgies the corner is out.
They this and why and in this bat
an eyelash to be better than that
on the day that.

And that was all a better than that day had that
unto the jousting which was unto a way down that.
They mortared the way under the man hat
that wanted to under a bill be that that.

In London just now is cold.
In London just now a gull spring
in London on the back of the bat
in London on the back of that.

When they and London remove the bat back
the bat backer became the bat back.
The butt packer begat the back pack
under lest the noise disturb those that bat back.

In the backing the true bat resides
under a cleft the cliff nose
gannets nosed underside.
The cliff-size size briar sizes up size,
decides size is lies under briar thighs.

That was a lot of that and lack
come down the stair decorum
and lack of reasonable store bin
under the store the straw was been.
Me like methink it all past being
and beyond into the been that he sinned,
the being that has seen
under the hedgerow greens as feline
is opposed to oppressed being been
and never two of us no no more we'll have been.

The barn exploded.
The big store ripped apart.
Gravel on the lawn made its mark
yes that and festoon of grit in the sky
while the riders came riding by
and nobody was appointed to fill the exam
no others why no other have ever been

why the irritated sky
and we'll never be the fly
not two states ever to fly by

and no more store no more in store by the fly
they fly by and take just as your daddy did
and stand by the chest

just make sure to be to the thigh
came crawling across clock's tempest.

LIKE AIR, ALMOST

It comes down to
so little:
the gauzy syntax
of one thing and another;
a pleasant dinner
and a frozen train ride into the exhaustible
resources.

We'd had almost enough,
tossing the cap to first one
and then the other one,
but still weren't determined
to give up the drive.
It had so much we wanted!
But besides that, was
fickle, overdetermined.

So I passed on that.
It was worth it.
Angelic eventide came along after afternoon,
a colibri fluttered questioning wings,
all so we might be taken out,
aired.

And when the post-climax happened
in soft shards, falling
this way and that,
signing the night's emeralds away,
we took it to be a sign of something.
"Must be a sign of something."
Then the wind came on, and winter with it.
"Why, weren't we just here,
five minutes ago?"
I thought I'd have another look,

but that way is all changed, and besides,
no one goes there anymore,
it's too popular.

Just one fragment
is all I ever wanted,
but I can have it, it's too much,
but its touch is for another time,
when I'm ready.

Crowd ebbs peacefully.
Hey it's all right.

THE BLESSED WAY OUT

Those who came closest did not come close.
The unknown leaned out to them,
then it was post-afternoon. Yes, Jerry built it.
There are many of them in Old Town.

What with one thing and another
you gave me all sorts of fur presents, you know.
It was good to come back. Gumball machines furnish
the library's stark living style.

You can't compete with what the
car tells its owner. One by one you are mortal
if the watershed idea catches on
and if we are credited for our utterance.

They thought serendipity was the most beautiful thing in the world.
They were right. As the wheel takes hold,
other inspirations spike it.

There was no year like it for taxation.
FDR decreed a large public works program
that had to be supported with funds from somewhere.
Inevitably, these took the form of taxation.

As when a redbreast calls, there is someone to hear it.
Calico got pasted over the mouse hole.
What are we doing in a theater more than one
wondered. Leaves fled like falling stocks.

SIGHT TO BEHOLD

The album sinks through fog, its unclasped pages
oozing afterthoughts: "If he weren't such a sacrificial lamb
we'd have been delivered sooner. As it is, he grasps at straws
or fluff to keep his conscience afloat, which, in any case, seethes
in the authorial chant of bees."

Don't make him jump through hoops, I heard another one say
of me. Hey, I was just getting down to business.
A cab appeared at the door, as though summoned.
That it gave me quite a turn I don't have to tell you.
You know you've arrived at bedlam when the arc lights
expire. Alternate-side-of-the-street parking has been suspended,
as has parking. Other than dishpan hands
I have naught to fondle you with. The memory eddies,
sinks, bobs up again, is carried away for good. Now,
what was I telling you? You're telling me. And beyond that point
of darkness, good citizens don't go. It's implanted
in their genes, to flower along the way. And a good job
it's not, old sod.

Like Knights Templar, we took our time, making sure
we were getting there. Sooner or later the proof dissolves
in the pudding. Made to look inconvenient, we had our say
again, and it was all profit and loss; the streets
had nowhere to go. We lived like nabobs, piling excess
on excess, till one fine day there was nothing left to wake up to.
I suppose it's for that we're being punished,
only this punishment is more like a thrill,
the slow beginning of a roller-coaster ride.
Be admonished then, but don't take
it too much to heart either. Their records need you and your kind.

PRISONER'S BASE

It might have made
Cindy's testimony
less credible,
and now seems at low ebb.

It may be just cold enough now.
Stars may have become polluted.
You go on your nerve.
Take no prisoners.
Fine. I don't want any prisoners
anyway I thought.
Stretched by history,
teething a new day,
what is convoluted gets to be convoluted,

and our brief passion left its scar,
firmly, on murk
which was OK until that other day.

Father of the bending serpents—

as they look back on the 21st century
what will *we* see?
Now he's retiring and she's retiring and their kids are retiring—
I say sir I don't feel

though I have never felt better.
Better to be the cusp of someone's tongue
and the materials of a new room begin arriving.

THE BUSINESS OF FALLING ASLEEP (2)

Par délicatesse j'ai perdu ma vie.
—Rimbaud

Days, things, times of day. Big things like unseen bells. Unheard moments. Suburbs are pale orange and a greenish blue I associate with fire escapes and school. The school looms now: a person with five questions at its back. They can't stay there, for now. They'll be back.

The interrogation was like a question mark. Once you stop to listen you're hooked. No, go back to the stone please. What did it say over the stone? Don't say I can't remember, you remember everything. That is true but I'll remember the stone

like the face of only the third dead person I'd ever seen. Well it's happened, he seemed to be saying. The eyes were closed (I suppose they always are). What are you going to do now? We don't have to stay like this. We could meet perhaps outside. Have a tea like we used to.

They moved the hotel boat to a less ostentatious location, still it felt hard coming to you through trees and other animated life. "Its music doesn't gel." Yes, but a weird creepy feeling came over me that you might know about all this, not wanted to tell me but just know. It's amazing how the past shrinks to the size of your palm, forced to hold all that now. Falling down the steps in Marlborough Street. That was just one thing, but others I don't know, never will know, are cupped in the hand as well. To brave the day turning outward like an ear, too polite to hear.

Rimbaud said it well, though his speech could be clamorous. One accepts that too within a broader parterre of accepting, a load of sun coming over the house to dampen discreet despair, woven into the togs of somebody standing up to go having remarked on the time as though there were a time to go. One would rather be left with few words and the resulting remainder of unease than never to have left the party.

Visions of a terrace with a cell phone ought to be engraved on the waiting skull, like Brahms. Anxious in the predicate but adept socially, pressure to have the music come out in a certain place, where it can be abandoned if desired. How about it? I care too much

not to leave it all. Set this down too . . .

REAL TIME

A merry-go-round reminds itself of flies,
listing dangerously in its element.
Thousands of years engrossed its sullen size.

In boiled wool and woolen lace, clockwise
our elders cinched a quad with ice o'ersprent
as merry-go-rounds bethought themselves of flies.

Glimpsed sharp in ragged dawn the old franchise
builds for us what they could have hardly meant.
Thousands of years engross its sullen size

that demon domestics haste to neutralize.
As in old flickers, laughs and colors blent
in a merry-go-round, doom themselves like flies—

though it's not urgent; there's time to entomologize.
We need only yawn, following the docent's
trail, and thousands of years engross our sullen size.

Age sags; little's left to elegize.
Waking from waltz-dream with time to repent
our merry-go-round bestirs itself, then flies.
Thousands of tears erode its sullen sides.

HEAVENLY DAYS

I

The philosopher walked over to me and tapped me on the brow
with his pencil. Now does *this* remind you of anything?
Have you ever seen anything like this before?
Yes, if it's in sync with the marrow of the growing world.
I can relate to that mattress. I do. I mean I do, sometimes.
And what day of the week might this be?
I'll make a wild guess—it's Thursday. You're wrong,
though it *seems* like a Thursday. They sent me the *Times*
upstream all the way, it arrived and began to smile, I
was startled, I always am when it's like that. But this
time it was different, more was at stake, though I don't know
what, exactly. More overtime, perhaps. Get
on with it, we don't have all night. You think
I like watching the candles gutter? Well, do you?
Yes, I think you do rather, but that's not the point.
Well what is the fucking point? It's that you were here,
earlier, and took too long to get here. By then
it was too late, but you'd been here earlier, hoping to cast
it as earlier, and yourself in a favorable light.
That light is now swaying from the chandelier, like an orangutan
awaiting further instructions, in mid-mischief, wondering if
all this is porridge after all. The philosopher is your boyfriend.
Remember you were hot before. Now it seems like an unseasonable crust,
with breath still to be counted, the weird smell,
and the way it all tallies with the trellis up the chimney.
You, on the other hand, were out of the country, or so you say,
and so couldn't possibly have witnessed the flare
that in fact no one saw, and can get on with it. My
conscience is clear. I'm hungry, and lunch, or supper, is waiting.

II
Between sleep and rubbish is the remembrance,
scent to one who can smell. What a relief, though—if snow flies
and they decide to walk back into it, that will make one more game.
Yes, *mon chou*, the way it is has been decided. When they come up for air
at the same moment, a truce is called,
and the staircase draped with shagreen. Others
than they may of course make decisions, but only in the infinity
of ways which concern us. We blacked out for a moment.

Still others avoid laxatives and beef. We cannot logically condone
headway in the matter. I said you brought back library books
that were due on June 23, 1924, and you owe me four trillion eight
    hundred
thousand twenty-three cents. Luckily a moratorium
was introduced in the last decade, forgiveness was invented,
and you are free to sulk by the ladder.

As it was I took the elevator to the top,
walked around and didn't see anything and came back down.
Then, acting on a hunch, I went up much faster
than the first time, and spotted two lovers entwined on the horizon,
but let them go, training the big bertha instead on a rabbit
limping across hallowed ground, was dismissed, took early retirement
    instead
to avoid embarrassment all round, and now am as you see me:
a blind cook serving pornographic muffins to paying guests
over cocktails before the sea opens and drinks us, then closes over us,
smacking its lips like an idiot.

III

Everything from soup to nuts is OK with me. Her bust came
buckled to Dad's breeches, someone in trouble.
Halving and having a new thing are the same.
I always preferred him, he was a wreck, superior to the common man,
but oh so separate. If he had dimples,
everybody had to have them. If he went to bed with someone
everybody else had to too. It was his summer of fun.
The fashions "dictated" a lot of things just then, we were cool
with that. Some of you might think of life as some kind of upper berth
on a honeymoon. Marriage on stilts. The absolute truth is,
no one's going to look at you once it's done.
We may as well refresh ourselves—the chase soon comes to a head,
though not for long, as Galileo's orange teaches.
The truth is always a bit further on, and sits there.
No one can read the expression
on its supplanted face.

The third monster seemed to think it was his turn to say something.
    "Well . . ."
"Folks I can't go on like this, that is, you can't.
Whoever suffers fate's naughty cudgel ought to come clean.
Otherwise there's no explanation, and that cannot be,
as we know. In some other life siphoned out of this one with a tube we can all
kiss our masters, for that day anything is play.
The raddled cowslips of diverted energy have a vested interest in us.
The team partly owns a share of each one of us. Go figure. Ask Neptune.
And insofar as I count, I'm lowering the iron shutter
on today's wares. God help us if he comes along. But if he doesn't
we shall be sisters all the same, tame in embroidery, yet resistant
where least expected. My dog speaks proof. I can ladle surf too,
I used to be a bathhouse attendant. I got good grades in math.
Didn't get into the college of my choosing. Oh well. It's triste,
the drain choked with tumbleweed, mascara on the clouds, the wooden
    false fronts

of our little downtown, only we hadn't left it this way, and ought not to
    foregather
as darkness falls and the real fur flies. You get caught out at night."
The girl in the drawing said it and made it happen to me,
then turned over.

The nexus of the star is a superbrain
that can take in you and me and not be mottled or disturbed,
while we lead quiet, shadowed lives. Insignificance is all we have.
The colors, dark ocean maroon, we belong to in the sense that earth
    belongs to us,
more reassurance, and when day collapses it's the same—a plight
that is a solution. That's why I can never go back to philosophy—
its halls and chambers are a paradigm of emptiness, not the real thing,
for only under stones is the knowledge
of underneath, and my desire is mammoth.
So it's decided. I'll pack my suitcase
or something, we have the tickets.

Someday I'll get you there, I know this, the flaming artery obstructs
but not that much, chestnuts still bask in the fire.
But when it came time to sample other essences
she had absconded, wasn't behind the goalpost.
In this way, rhizome-like, life gets added to life until there is no backing
    down,
and again tackles its dull awareness of today's
not remembering our names, only faces.

But there's no mistaking their intent.
The missile had locked on its prey, houses are swept
for weddings, they cry and can't alter anything.
We each had an appetizer, the pupils left.
My tetrahedron is open to the night.

("But was it hinted that brains slant otherwise?
That a draft of cunning will get you into the fair,
where, as long as you keep quiet, you can own great, quivering beasts?
That one's breath on the moat ignores the shoulders of pike,
and once more the canon desires what it devours,
made to come round again? That we were cousins once in Duluth?
That there is scrimping out there where buzzards plow
the greenery and bellboys interrupt? I'll be my own vast placebo.
Twilight comes with a rush and wet plumbing.
There is more to our story, more to the telling of it—")

The unbuilt demands added attention. We got swept along,
and you never learned Jay's last name. Perhaps it was Jay.
Evening ebbed on the hour.
The newspaper arrived by pigeon post,
as might be. We loved hot food. There is something else
for you and me. Sighed the voyante. And they wonder why it didn't
taste just right. With dead milk. But surely that
was an inning, it had to be. We had all worked so hard. It comes over me,
all this loss, and then the time. Added to your hours. For a few thrilling
    minutes
she came and sat by us. "For now, it's all right. The children would have
    wanted
you to be this way, happy. But the older I get the harder
it is for me to climb the giant root,
beyond which is an extension of everything, see? You do see.
I'll leave you the latchkey, at last. Don't hesitate to use it.
Don't call me. Or see anything wrong with this." Like a charming
serpent, she took her leave, with one half of us in suspense,
the other clotured. But it was turning out this way. I knew it all
along, in the hallway of your dwelling. You shouldn't make such noises
and not mean them. There'll come a day when we'll live off noise,
but for now the square forecourt is overgrown. I've loved some things in
    my time,

cast others aside, let others fall by the wayside. The feast such
as we now reap it is heavy, indistinct. Their voices blur. They could croon.
Each to the other thinks: It's gone. But rotten. Days will
go on turning themselves inside out for us, and trees warble for us,
but not often and not very well.

SIR GAMMER VANS

Last Sunday morning at six o'clock in the evening as I was sailing
over the tops of the mountains in my little boat a crew-cut stranger
saluted me, so I asked him, could he tell me whether the little old
woman was dead yet who

was hanged last Saturday week for drowning herself in a shower of
    feathers?
"Ask Monk Lewis what he thinks 'been there done that' means in the so-
    called
evening of life. Chances are he'll regale you with chess moves. All I
want is my damn prescription." "And you shall have it, *sir*," he answered
in a level voice. So he gave me a slice of beer and a cup of cold veal
and there was this little dog.

I see no reason to be more polite when the sun has passed its zenith,
yet ham radio operators infest every cove, defacing walls with their
    palaver.
And when two swans come to that, one swoons and is soothed.
The other lost inside a wall.

He seemed to think I knew some secret or other pertaining to the botched
logs in the fireplace. This caused him to avoid me I think
for a twelvemonth.
After which we got down to business and actually signed the contract.
He was inconsolable. The brat had cost him. With two wives and another
on the way wouldn't commit himself to a used Chevy. Which is
understandable I think I said it's understandable. The man
was in no mood to entertain these distinctions. At least I thought he said
bring on the heavy artillery the dream is now or
it won't happen, not in my diary. Well why that's just what
I think too, I blessed him. Cells in the wind. The sucker'll be all
over our new templates, smearing them with grape honey, I'll
challenge you for the right to beleaguer. To which he assented
abstractedly and it was over in a thrush. Not to . . . well excuse me

too. Curses I'd already signed on,
there was no need to jump for it, put a good face on it. Mild eyes
expressing a child's dignity. OK for it to rot, it
was pompous to begin with.

"No, don't hang him," says he, for he killed a hare yesterday. And if you
don't believe me I'll show you the hare alive in a basket.

So they built a pontoon bridge, and when they had crossed over the fish
    applauded.
I was aghast, lost forty pounds at the gaming tables of the
Channel Islands, 'sblood I said. So I set fire to my bow, poised my arrow,
and shot amongst them. I broke seventeen ribs on one side,
and twenty-one and a half on the other; but my arrow passed clean
    through
without ever touching it, and the worst was I lost my arrow;

however I found it again in the hollow of a tree. I felt it; it felt
clammy. I smelt it; it smelt honey.